VOLCANO VERSES

Also by H. A. Fergus

POETRY

Calabash of Gold, Linda Lee Books, 1993
Lara Rains and Colonial Rites, Peepal Tree Press, 1998
Volcano Song: Poems of an Island in Agony, Macmillan, 2000

HISTORY AND SOCIETY

Montserrat: Emerald Isle of the Caribbean, Macmillan, 1983
Montserrat: History of a Caribbean Colony, Macmillan, 1994
Gallery Montserrat: Prominent People in Montserrat's History, UWI Press, 1996
History of Education in the British Leeward Islands 1838-1945, UWI Press, 2003

EDITOR

The Sea Gull and Other Stories, With V. J. Grell, UWI Montserrat, 1976
Hugo Versus Montserrat, With E. A. Markham, Linda Lee Books, 1989
Eruption: Montserrat Versus Volcano, UWI Montserrat, 1996

HOWARD A. FERGUS

VOLCANO VERSES

P E E P A L   T R E E

Peepal Tree Press Ltd
17 King's Avenue
Leeds LS6 1QS
First published in 2003

ISBN 1-900715-79-1

ACKNOWLEDGEMENTS

The poems 'A Minute Silence', 'Sideshow' and 'No Birthday Poem'
were originally published in *The Caribbean Writer*, Volumes 14 (2000)
and 15 (2001), and some others in *The Montserrat Reporter*. Earlier
versions of 'Two Men on the Streatham Road' and 'In Memory' have
appeared in earlier collections.

The clerical staff at the UWI Centre was responsible for typing the
manuscript.

Cover photograph by H. O. Woolcock

Peepal Tree gratefully acknowledges Arts Council support

For my Teachers: Vio, Josie, Elice, Elaine
and Jim Osborne

CONTENTS

3. OCCASIONAL POEMS

PREFACE

Since 1995 the people of the British Overseas Territory of Montserrat have been living with an erupting volcano. It roared into life in August that year and has danced to its unique rhythm of explosion, suspicious calm and dome collapse ever since. Tragedy struck in 1997 when fiery avalanches rushed down its flanks and killed 19 persons some at work in fields and others at rest in their homes (officially in the exclusion zone). A massive collapse on Boxing Day in the same year obliterated some southern villages, but fortunately these had already been evacuated.

The eruption led to a national crisis; there was mass migration scattering over half of the population of the 39.5 square mile island all around the world; the habitable space shrank by two-thirds and the economy collapsed. It is not difficult therefore to understand why the volcano has dominated the consciousness of Montserratians including its writers for over half a decade. Political and social life centres largely around the volcanic crisis and the very resilience of the people; and their efforts to remain and rebuild add to the romance of the island story.

Physically the soufriere towers over the island with its contrasting faces of beauty and ugliness; and its occasional drizzle or deluge of ash is an abiding reminder of its presence. Its columns of ash mushrooming towards heaven, its fires glowing like a city at night and the lava rushing down hillsides in fervent heat at break-neck speed are awesome as well as awful. But there is sometimes an ugliness about its craggy countenance with its rash of carbuncles. All this, together with the human drama – the engineering of new life, new localities and new relationships is a rich source of inspiring material, and song writers, dramatists and creative writers have had an inexhaustible field day.

This new ferment is further enriched by the new governance relationships with the British administration especially with its aid-dispensing arm, the Department for International Development (DFID). Several references are made in these poems to the DFID Minister Clare Short who in a now infamous remark asserted that the people of Montserrat were expecting golden elephants. A 2000

Christmas festival calypsonian vows to 'vote for DFID' at the next elections, since it is they supposedly who wield real power in the wasted isle. One result of the crisis was a relapse into grant-in-aid status from which the island had graduated some years before.

The stage had been already set for a 'disaster literature' following Hugo, one of the most devastating tropical hurricanes of the century. This led to the first major creative work on disaster, *Hugo Versus Montserrat* edited jointly by Professor E. A. Markham of Sheffield Hallam University and this author in 1989. Markham followed up with *Letter from Ulster & The Hugo Poems* (1993) in which he foresaw an active future for the volcano:

> Was here in '24
> Was here in '28
> Will be here the day Soufriere...
> Vomit corruption back in we face.

My own *Volcano Song: Poems of an Island in Agony* (Macmillan, 2000) is explicitly about the volcanic experiences but not exclusively, since there are other areas of life that still exercise the creative imagination. The present companion volume is similarly conceived, for island life and folk will outlast volcanic tantrums. The volcano may occupy centre stage but normal life is proceeding and there are sideshows – like cattle egrets showing off at horseback riding:

> Tonight Chances pique still grows
> An unholy dome still glows
> But cattle low and egrets ride
> In spite of fire from mountain tides.

This is the spirit of this book.

Howard A. Fergus

1: VOLCANO VERSES

NO BIRTHDAY POEM
25.6.2000

I will not sing Soufriere a birthday song
for this inauspicious day in June when birth
and death walked hand in hand on farms
at Farms and Farrells garnering rhizomes
from shallow graves among the furrows.
Rather write of four flamboyant trees,
defiant, flanking the Sahara of the west
at Belham river waving bunches of red smiles.
Good for you to take a stand in this land
where your roots are; you did not pull up
and run in spite of nineteen brothers dead
on their feet and numerous others fled
to watered valleys and pastures green with snow –
better than those mango trees, your neighbours,
gone with their sweetness and bowel-moving
properties, leaving our island constipated,
stuffed with intestine strife and ashes.

You are an inspiration to other persons
of the trauma, like these breadfruit trees
breeding under primitive conditions in full
glare of Soufriere, like shelterees in churches
where every deed is naked to the eyes
of God and children. Although producing mouths
to feed figures in His master plan.
Here where cotton blossomed and cane arrows waved
golden locks in trade winds like an offering,
and products took direct flight from black banks
at Farms and Farrells to the Bank of England
without passport or hindrance at the king's command,
even weeds struggle to survive – though vices
and small donkeys with big ears look green with promise.

On this ebb tide of desiccated river bones,
windswept gullies and a famine for rain,
you are not quite in your former glory
when your beauty was the song of story
in a flattered paradise, but your warm red hands
still beckon and homeless birds still shelter
in your eaves shadowing this desert sand.

No, I will not sing Soufriere a birthday song
for this infamous day at Farms and Farrells;
rather hymn emergent bowers braving
a flamboyant smile among the waste at Belham
river, Sahara of the Emerald Isle.

WARNING SHOTS

Yesterday scientists suddenly fired
another warning shot
across the battered bow of Montserrat

like the mysterious sound
of clouded thunder
and you wonder

why this volcano resurrection
couldn't wait at least three years
why this easter of our fears

came round so unexpectedly
to catch us and our prophets napping
like a thief of midnight coming.

The message swiftly darkened
white-cuffed waves of our new
normality and we wondered if the few

who stayed would be called upon
to pay for their wise
stupidity. Is this the prize

for standing on the burning deck
when cat and dog had fled
to England – our patriotism in the red

of Soufriere's anger? Were the jobs
we stayed to launder
from the ashes, prime time squandered?

Let me be wrong, Lord, but I pray,
preserve the hapless hulk of Montserrat
so that scientists may fire other warning shots.

VOLCANO WATCH

August 1995

Dearly beloved, we are gathered together
again on a solemn occasion,
on the brink of an infernal volcano,
brothers and sisters in calamity,
in this watch night service, hoping
morning comes without the night.
The journey still long, the sulphur strong
and the dangers unforeseen. Never mind
the multiple observatory posts
and the feverish *multi-ologist* scene,
we have come by faith just beyond Belham river
in obedience to God, Government
and the Governor's emergency powers
which are *ultra vires* with volcanoes.
We have come to pitch our camp at Olveston,
a sometime English village;
the winds at Gerald's Bottom are too strong
for our frail earthly tents.
In this storm-shocked island our Defence
Force must build for forever like love.

Pity our cats and dogs cannot gather
with us. Lines have to be drawn somewhere –
at rivers, soufrieres, great houses or mosques.
Nothing like carnivals and eruptions
to forge unity and fix boundaries.
There is no safety zone for our animals,
no curfew served on our curs;
they will fend for themselves at the expense
of the neighbour's sheep scattered like their shepherds
all over the land, battening in brown pastures.

Our bananas yellow and fall to the ground
(in this slippery season, government
learns to dodge hot ash and banana skins).
Our bowels of mercy yearn for our goats;
their water breaks prematurely
and they cannot kid death; some are wantonly
killed by dogs, inappropriately dressed
for send-off like our loved ones,
dead and buried in untidy haste
without wake, no drink on their heads.

But we have something to thank God for;
here in Olveston trees are still green;
there is no dust or ashes beyond the river.
I watch mangoes mellowing in August,
a little late in season; Soufriere ripening
in a hurricane; God's cup of mischief
fulling up fulling up. The people's elect
and Her Majesty's legate counsel calm recurrently,
exercising voice control. And Rose,
ZJB's voice without a thorn, pitched
high above the storm, plays telephone numbers
with sweet-smelling words and doleful songs
of hope – *Don't you worry about a thing*
Every little thing gonna be alright –
counselling us to cope and remain calm
on true religion without rum, drunk
in the house of God, the unseen host
at every meal, who offered us asylum.

With a puff and a blow Soufriere opened up
big craters in the economy, currency in flames,
but new occupations fall out
on the volatile market. Choppers paddle
through our skies, cutting through the Queen's
peace and tourist paradise,

17

telephones take on a shrill tone like sirens;
officials say that the scientists say...
and the isle is full of secondhand noises.
Helicopters search volcanoes for intelligence,
practise rescue in an emergency
in the face of clouds protesting
the violation of their air space
on Chances peak. A corps of scientists knock
heads, peep through instruments, plot graphs
to bring us comfort and despair in new tongues
with local echoes. Montserrat media
learnt the lingo fast and before the second
Cow Hill blast, tiltmetres, magma and phreatic
thoughts were flying through the air thick
like Chances mists obscuring light.
LIAT, flying in the cloud of our fears,
made gold from volcanic ash, ferrying
us to Antigua *en route* to anywhere
in return for instant cash.

We naturally could not get blue in the face
but saw red at the news that Royal
and Barclays had fled abroad to insure
their person and our cash. Perhaps.
They caused us to devalue our decision
to bank on them to bail us out in a jam.

Not so Rams, the nation's Indian mart,
always a smart businessman. He did not wish
to make capital out of disaster
or risk being the first volcanic martyr;
he only helped the people as his custom
to build a grocery store and run to red
alert in fat security, while he saved their cash.

In these serious times, in this narrow corridor
of safety, men still find space for speed
(in vehicles I mean). Brains go into over-
drive and death takes over, a tragic interlude
in volcano watch. I wonder will they pin
the crime on Soufriere on circumstantial
evidence alone? Even here in the house
of God tempers get hot and *expressions*
crack for the whip of our tongues.

As we gather again in this fashion
on volcano's edge, hope Soufriere doesn't play
hide and seek and come like Christ
as a thief in the night to give us hell.
Some of us plan to storm the rock
until the molten end, however strong
the shock, and build again from ashes.

SEVENTH ANNIVERSARY
1996

Strange I should forget
this sabbath of anniversaries.
A respite from demonic winds,
not years, has done the mischief;
but a white rose waved a semaphore
of praise through my battered window
and I remembered Hugo.

Storm clouds responded with a joy-
ful round of distant thunder
and charged the sky with telegraphic
codes of light to celebrate survival.
For on this anniversary, a God
who cannot rest is in cahoots with fire.
To the great shock of red-hot winds
and water, volcano gets the cake.
I'll be damned if I forget.

VOLCANO VESPERS

As the sun sets tonight,
Cow Hill soufriere sends up
columns of incense
to make a tabernacle of praise;
geysers are hot for God
and craters glorify Him
in a loud voice, grateful
for power to try Tar River
and Long Ground by fire,
tampering with judgement.

But you can't fool people
in the east with a display
of piety upon a high place.
They number their days,
testing God's temperature
to butter Him with a season of praise.
And when de rite time comes
He shall be pleased to shut the mouth
of dragons who breathe fire
and brimstone in high places.

And the Almighty shall dam
the rivers of lava, controlling
their flow, meting out mischief
with an even hand
in the streets of confusion
all over the land. He shall damn
vents in high places
as the sun sets all over the land
and Tar River and Long Ground
shall dawn like gold.

A MINUTE SILENCE
24.5.1999

1

Only the rhythm of the wind
creaming ashes like a blender
and the waves of a neurotic sea
pummelling her bleeding front.

Only the scattered patter of rain,
as from a parsimonious sender
dropping deadbeat in the sand,
no echo from the ceiling of the trees.

2

This once loquacious little town
is now forever silent
or on a long fast for speech;
no more hallucinatory snores
no love's loud ecstacy
no pulse. Plymouth is comatose
or dead.

Where taxi tempers flared
and drivers cursed each other's
mother's red light road,
a long sabbath of silence reigns.
There is posthumous forbearance now
for the city's seamy sidewalks.

The screaming smell of frying fish
pop-corn's scatter shots
the sizzle of chicken's flesh –
not native born or naturalized
but sweet like the sin of cholesterol –

are silent and doors to the capital
closed off like a crime scene.

Red meat writhing on a spit
to titillate salivary glands,
sate buccaneering appetites,
no longer solicits
just the marrow of history.

We had begun to savour curry
extra hot from those Guyana women
cooking iguanas and men's heads
in Indian pepper pots. The technology,
happily, trecked from south to north,
so no need to curry favour
for the aphrodisiac broth.

And Miss Rachel's black pudding —
feast and fetish of blood,
though thicker than water — crossed
over the flood to turn up the stomachs
of Christians (like the boat to Antigua)
who too far right of centre
and washed up in blood
made yokes of the word
barbed with commas and stops
like tyrants for teachers
whipping crosses and dots;
but belly fires still burn
for the black pudding pot.

3
O-gad-o-lards at the fishermen's bar
no longer mix and mingle
with hell-fire hallelujahs
preaching peace and new wine at the War

23

Memorial: the weft and colour of culture
buried under Soufriere's dung
from years of constipation.

The bang bang of the ice plant,
an anvil beating giant ice blocks
into shape to shelter us from thirst,
a sound of the past,
the exact location of its sepulchre
forever lost.

The bruising grate of shaven ice
with syrupy blood to cool the pain
in a travelling *freco* factory
no longer blunts internal fires.

The crack of cow-hide whips
on masquerade roads,
like wake-up calls on the backs of slaves,
has lost its lash
leaving only music's silent footfall.

The chop of machetes
walking through meat at the chatter-box
market, mincing the neighbour's reputation
in a rumour mill, powdered by sulphur,
has rusted. The bellow of cattle mercilessly killed
is over; the crime of cruelty to animals
suspended.

4
Ships that dropped in frequently
to ease their bowels
pass by, no flags of respect,
no look of familiarity,

like ungrateful comrades when your fortune
falls. Just a distant drone of engines and a piddling
ripple to mock the town's mortality.

5
I tried, head bowed, a minute's mark
of silence – just a minute of respect
for a lost loved one,
but the sea and deafening silence
of the scenery stranded my efforts
at just a minute of respect.

Perhaps a party to sugar coat
the silence, feast the dead, an African rite
reconditioned in America,
like laundered cars, value-added for export.
But be careful with the table-setting
in this joyous house of mourning.
Pass up cold briefcase advice
for just a minute;
death and dying knowledge is the heritage
of creole intelligence.

The party over, like a Town Hall
ball at midnight, the lapel
dance with lipstick brushed aside
to greet the Sunday rising
in apparently white apparel,
I will attempt another mark of silence,
while the sea sleeps from night-time
overhang, for just a minute of respect,
just a minute...

ACROSS THE RIVER
21.8.1999

I see grins of glory etched
beautifully on mahogany faces now;
they integrate in bars and churches,
hum like bees in business places,
they hammer hard on rooftops,
driving nails to build a Christmas
in their coffins of despair.

Green trees and green houses
are erupting in the deserts of the North
to the steel music of mattocks,
and songs of the millennium
have begun to gild our rocks.

I see grins of glory dawning
on my people's faces now
and I shake a leg with them,
kiss glasses in a toast of jubilation,
glad to be alive on the other side
of trial and the tossing of the flood.

PARADISE AGAIN?
20.10.1999

This Olveston garden is a possible post view
of the true paradise. Pardon the cliché,
but the prime ambition of every oriole backyard
dashed with blue is to climb back into Eden
some illegal way, slipping the steep religious
roundabout. But we were squarely driven out
and perhaps fairly. In this case there was no
House of Higher Lords or Clintonian senate
for an appeal from that first instance; tyranny
was good governance (more cliché), with naked
men arraigned at a primeval bench planted
in a garden – an idyllic setting
for a draconian sentence. I cannot censure God
but he was judge and jury *extraordinaire.*
I open no wise cracks on who will try the guardian
whose cranium is a master calabash of wisdom.

There was no forceripe show of force for eating
a silly apple to make you wise – for cultural
taste a hairy mango would be sweeter.
No *tonton macoute,* or *mongoose gang* to seal off
the property in question; it was an elite palace
guard, an angel with a no-nonsense sword
and razor-sharp demeanour. To hell with those
who testify that God is not a merciful
environmentalist of taste; he could have made
Eden an exclusion zone by torching a volcano
stoned with gas as he did in Montserrat,
creating waste. Innocence, like maidenhead,
was ruptured in the garden with just a hint of blood.
No hurricane Jose-fiend blew and blustered
to burn and blight the garden like an extravagant
politician breathing out power. Eve did the damage

under cover of her natural petticoat. Adam ate
the apple from her lap and lost the real estate.

Mine is just a green reflection of the prototype
made in man's image and, by the extended family,
God's. I am insured against expulsion
thanks to the right royal William Henry Bramble
who annulled the stolen deed of tenancy eviction at Tuitts
and Long Ground and broke the ferula of distant rule.
I have a good deed and a duly signed certificate.
That snake, sinuous and subtly painted,
which makes this yard authentic, is my own;
it is a creeping thing that cannot intercourse
with man or fool him with the coalition politics
of a smart-ass woman, with child for good and evil.

There is no alien apple here, but soursop
and sugar apple, too delicate for Europe's palate,
have survived the envious winds of Josephine.
I wonder what mysterious undergrowth of healing
herbs bloom within this garden, camouflaged
by purple bougainvillaeas studded with thorns,
red exoria, saffron rose, pink poincianas,
perfumed bowers – nature's carnival of colours
in a diplomatic dance to baffle Babylon, putting him
off scent. What barks to sap for wisdom?
What leaves to tap for aphrodisiac properties,
or libido's longevity? How read the runes
of twisted roots to lift the curse of paradise
and iron out arthritis? I may have happed upon
a holy place not half, I hope, as ominous as Eden,
and without the penance of a new epiphany.

SECOND COMING
17.3.2000

Waiting for the spill of the anger
of the mountain is like waiting for a second

coming. Come it must, but no one, not the mountain,
knows the hour of dome collapse, the magic moment

of apocalypse. Will it ride on ash-grey
horses or in chariots of fire? Will it merely

come to pass defiant babels in the North
or will it light new funeral pyres at Bethel?

Will it come, as at St. Patrick's, a bonus
for epiphany, a thief just after Christmas night,

or noonday as at Molyneaux and Paradise
robbing wretched workers of the light?

Either way, it is to the same sources that we pray
for a dignified send off. Either way. Calm seas

at Carrs Bay, clear air at the heliport.
We wait upon the mercies of Jehovah and Clare Short.

DFID

23.5.2000

As acronyms and bureaux go
Dfid is not difficult, though slow

on project uptake and the double d
a wee bit clumsy. It doesn't differ

definitely from imperial pursers
down the years, though in the after-

math of cotton and Soufriere, their lengthy
procedures draw more blood and tears.

Dfid is not indifferent to the plight
of Montserrat or diffident to pay,

except there is a genuine impediment.
Good team players, they are dependable

in a shortfall – witness the white elephant
at Brades – and they have the brazen art

to call a spade a spade. They are
loyal to their mistress, defender of the

minimalist mercies of the honourable short
and they keep you hanging only for the sport.

Dfid is not difficult as imperial bureaux go
just mercilessly accurate and generously slow.

A LITTLE LONELY
13.7.2000

A vigorous walk round Old Towne and Olveston,
the circle where big boys used to play,
is a stimulating exercise
of the imagination if you put your heart in it;
you see houses living near the sea
(a little lonely) with pools that bring a private
sea inside the house. Gardens still grin at you
through the ashes with an occasional cattle.
Trespass and pound have all evacuated,
leaving grey-white pages on the statute book
as vacant as the house. Big gardens,
ripe for baseball fields, if you have a mind for it,
look a little lonely. Windows are locked
behind cold bars of adamantine steel
against the blow of this *unarctic* winter
without snow, against the soufriere creep
that steals and corrupts properties. A little sad,
not even a toppled garbage bin
disturbs the peace and humours vermin.

These houses are not walk-in luxuries,
just the right size if you new reside
in a tropic paradise under a British sky
with hardly any serpents in the grass –
just shy agoutis with unfinished tails
that give a fleeting glimpse of life and colour
to the unruffled bed of peace. They, too, look a little lonely.

A dog, on part time, barks staccato
in the distance, just to impress or for the exercise;
too little industry for full time occupation
when robbery and rape do not penetrate the peace.

Soufriere has stolen canine thunder
and pulled the teeth of their ferocity. They bow-wow
out of boredom, being a little lonely.

Old Towne and Olveston are not alabaster cities
any more. A walk across this gilded ghetto,
through fields where big boys used to play,
can be a depressing exercise. You can gain weight,
or wonderment, if you put your heart in it.

SEPTEMBER 17

17.9.2000

I dread September 17 more than the hugest
hurricane or a full sack of teenage pregnancies
of girls whose mothers and grandmothers fell
on a forceripe date in like steamy circumstance;
or the cloven tongues of soufriere licking
its chops at nineteen bodies on a spit.
What if bloodless houses get beheaded here
and there; it's the calendar witchcraft that I fear.

I dread September 17 more than the mental
patients who tramp unshod our one-way roads,
back and forth and to and from, in this almost
British isle without a south or sunny east or cities
built for refuge. Not means-tested for an outside chance
of an inside toilet, they release an instant gush
with a fig-leaf sense of privacy – no zip humbug,
no liquid soap, designer drawers or Avon scent.
Big people stare and children bellyful their eyes.
But what if cocoa brown floodwaters flush
polluted ghauts and deluge leaking Noah's arks
to give contrary politics an honourable house of talk;
it's at the uncanny number that I balk.
For those unhappy chances never might have been
but for that 'knock-wood' number seventeen.

SIDESHOW
(for denville 18.10.2000)

A tasty decoration
like a candle on a cake,
a technicolour postcard
of professional make,
or nature's own networking
only beggarly describe
an egret's stand-up stunt ride
on a willing cattle back
and 'bull and bird in circus' sounds
like a metaphor for clowns.

It was a moving picture
in the waning light,
a bid to steal the focus
from the spires of Soufriere
misting like a ganja sacrifice
and the smoking of a prayer.

Cattle back was a cultural centre
for the white egret, its verandah theatre
under the stars – a spot to socialize
and be refreshed. When combing cattle
for tick, a hardly altruistic act,
this was the place to pause.

The sideshow was a peaceful contrast
while it lasted; not just white on red,
big bearing small, but an object lesson
in coexistence at the instep of a mountain
which holds a land in thrall.

Tonight Chances pique still grows,
an unholy dome still glows,
but cattle low and egrets ride
in spite of fire from mountain tides.

BELOVED ISLAND

Those whom the gods love die young
17.12.2000

The preacher claims that God loves Montserrat –
a bitter pill, but with troubles multiplying
I will blindly swallow that.

The nineteen barbecued unevenly whom 'God loved best'
is a childhood orthodoxy I would faithfully reject,
but in this bunkered dispensation, Yes.

The mountains have come down and spoken
with granite authority: let Plymouth close
and what we shut no Brand can open.

No abbot or Clare Short is equal
to Soufriere's awesome power to convert;
the Belham river rose into a valley of Ezekiel.

And do not underrate the flood
that loves our land in triple mode, drowning Noah's
with fiery avalanches, rocks and coffee mud.

Like father, son and holy ghost in concord,
they sing in rounds like children about
the loving wrath of a tri-partisan God.

The preacher claims that Montserrat has its fill
of God's love, seeing hell at morning.
I screw my face and take the pill

like blacks swilling white rum, no chase,
heads thrown back to down the potent medicine,
a heady mix of joy and discomfort in the face.

MISSION
19.12.2000

Strange irony that those who came
Columbus-like to prove that Montserrat
was still spinning round the sun,
and give the lie to scared adventurers
and the perilous spin of the BBC
on eyewitness testimony, made landfall
on a sober truth. The door from the Antigua
side, the only side in this one-sided
island, was slammed shut by an evil
wind that blew the land no good;
same wind that blew hell fires underneath
the copper boilers of Soufriere
with choice anger like a god's.
Too polite for such tasteless turbulence
the *Opale Express* could not do battle
with the waves which once Britannia
ruled with scant resistance, and the gulf
between the island and the outside world
is too dangerously deep for progress
without bigger British bottoms and smiling
native harbours. The seas at Little Bay
have no respect for white or black
when they get drunk at Christmas time;
their words will spot-a-dash a saint.
It was a crash course in patience
with on-shore perils in Antigua
from vocal swells, billows of frowning
foreheads and trips over baggage
like an obstacle race. Eggs of a wintry
reception messing up your face.
Poorer for the forced delay by stormy
doldrums in Antigua they arrived
without a mutiny of wind and water

in spite of threats (Intelligence on the reception
at Little Bay is classified). The evening
breath is warm and they will after all return,
their love of home as lasting as the 'Little
Town of Bethlehem' though Plymouth burns.

NICE
22.12.2000

Montserrat nice
Still paradise
in spite of the fall
of the tall mountain –
if you are fixed with wings
like angels;
and there are saving graces:
the isle is full of noises
from ancient drums of masquerade
and the constant din
of battle over British aid;
the list of shortages
is shorter now;
and you can readily access
toilet paper from the not so friendly
wharf in allied Antigua;
carols and calypsoes compete
in dead heat for the king;
babies are born to provide us
with more mouths to feed
and more books hard to read;
politicians still get elected via ballot;
words wound and kill
but they are not exactly bullets.

Montserrat nice
Still paradise
in the imagination
of poets and calypsonians
in search of life
with painless rhymes.

TRUCE

23.12.2000

The volcano is under orders from the bridge
(I don't mean Belham bridge, that is the limit)
to yield our narrow living room
to gratify the visitors. Brought up on heat
it wouldn't be uncomfortable in the kitchen.
Ash is a local product but it isn't snow
and import substitution has its bounds;
appearance is important too.

It's not that we are ashamed of you.
You are not poor family but our future
trump to trap adventurers who love
to plumb tantrums thrown by nature
in its nastier mood, until its godly
temper cools; but high on gas, you spill
your guts in every gully and hang out
your dirty clothes on every tree
ignoring high class protocol and common hospitality.

The volcano is no estate slave; it gets red hot
with rage at pressure from inferior management.
Living in a crown land sanctuary
it knows its rights and threatens to erupt
unless the order comes from higher up,
direct from England. No prince consort, worse still
Clare Short, for since this sceptred isle is colony
it bows to nothing short of summit majesty.

But we are reasonable in this little
emerald isle and sweeter having grown up
under cane. You may pity our simplicity
but we have better things to kill for
than orange streets, weeping walls and west banks.
We planted orange among sugar banks
and built stone walls to shore up terraces.
Sources close to Soufriere say that she is not opposed
to reason and is open to negotiation of a truce,
in the first place, for a season; and most times
you can trust the *verilys* of scientists
except those trained by the narrow channels of the BBC.

SHOW TIME
25.12.2000

The volcano must be family
to some people that I know;
it's as temperamental and dramatic –
always loves to steal the show.
We have come to Christmas morning
without alarm or siren calls,
just a blowing of the nose
and a clearing of the throat –
Soufriere joining the contagion
of that cold going about.
You are conscious of the poses
of the mountain, like those folks
who cough to draw attention
to their entrance to a room. Invited
or uninvited, Soufriere can spoil a party.

I hope it does not leap up on stage,
give an unforgettable display
as it did in '97 on Boxing Day.
But do not hold your breath – except for fear
of drizzling ash and catching fever
from Soufriere. With this volcano
nothing's ever over until it is all over.

VOLCANO AUDIT
27.12.2000

The Lord giveth and the Lord taketh away
with full immunity to *cat boils*. This is not a dead
philosophy. Copycat landlords lacking
industry lent their lands and pushed the bounds
of usury beyond all recognition.

They hijacked black people's cotton to cover
redness with impunity in spite of
canons extant against exorbitance
in a liberal dispensation where breasts
of human kindness did not cup in ample size.

We were tall on checks and check points, but short
on balances and false scales shared our cotton.
We lost on the fine details in the real
estate deal at Tar River and Trants.
God and Soufriere credited us with plates,

oven-hot to sizzle instant fish, but even
deserts find it hard to grow in these new lots;
and only diehard tourists fixed with wings
and stoned on natural exotica will be passing
there for years. They took away Bramble

that flew in up to forty in a dash
and gave us rude seas, toys and novelties:
a chopper and a heliport for the middle
passage to Antigua at a high price –
the mortgage of a flying future.

In a rare fit of generosity they took
away our fertile south and signed us up on welfare
but we did not fare well. It was goodbye
to comfortable beds. Like Soufriere, we suffered
a change of colour – our culture is in the red.

OPENNESS
2.1.2001

The volcano has learnt to keep its secrets
well these several months.
The scientists, with all their claim
to inside intelligence, cannot truly tell
when a dome collapse will come to pass.
The volcano dances to its own music;
and no mole lives on the mountain.

It signals smoke on occasions,
and you swear there's fire behind.
Dark clouds gather overhead but the rain –
no, drizzle – is mild;
clearing follows like a mocking smile.
Judging from the antics of this creature,
man has heights to go to fully fathom nature.

I wonder will it crack in the new year
spilling its insides
in a dramatic show of openness.
No need then for scientific hieroglyphics
for a season. In plain language
All of us will know.

UPDATE: NO SIGNIFICANT CHANGE
(After a T-Shirt)

The island is still paradise;
you occasionally smell the hell
of soufriere and brimstone and fire
sweep down the slopes of our myth
to sculpt a new hieroglyph
in the lee of the land
but the island is nice.

Temperature choking to mild –
occasionally red-hot, volcano's
own child. We lean on England's cold
shoulder to weather the rocks;
we slip and we slide sometimes fall
through the cracks but is still paradise
and our mother is nice.

A season of ash brings spice
to our lives; it occasionally hails
mad manna from heaven
a plague on our houses
instead of a feast but at least
there is pause for an update
while you sweep, sweep to keep
the clean of our myth
and the island is nice

Custom-made 'ologists' up-market doctors
with long-distance thermometers
monitor the health of soufriere;
they bid us move to its music
occasionally frantic; its terrific
son et lumière is ever so inviting.
Have no fear, the island is nice.

2: PEOPLE

THE CHARCOAL MAN

He was all of seven feet tall;
his torso firm, his tread was sure;
his arms and calves were stout and strong;
size fourteen was his shoe or more.

He climbed Jo Morgan Hill at dawn
spurring a burry donkey mane;
he was a king among the woods,
unflattered by a rabble train.

Yielding to him, the forest groaned,
fearing each keen machete stroke
as he deadly havoc wrought
'mongst guava, birch and Spanish oak.

Pausing, he spoke with clarity,
voicing a grim philosphy:
Life is a struggle.

Mopping his broad and sweaty brow,
he cocked his cap now black with grease,
loosed his necktie-belted waist
and went aside himself to ease.

The sun's hot rays now riding high
beckoned time for the descent.
His belly rumbled emptily
to signal inner strength was spent.

To urge the overloaded ass
to cruise along the faithful track,
he sang him a domestic tune
of grass and cornstalk in a sack.

From a wood-pile by a pit latrine
resinous mists like incense rise
and children in a chorus cried,
'The coal-pit of Man-Dight, the wise'.

For ever he would faithfully
visit his grim philosphy:
Life is a struggle.

In three days when the coal was burnt,
the smoke was low, the smell was pure;
from coal-black lips his ivory teeth
grinned that his bread was hard, but sure.

Into the town at a jaunty trot,
he needed neither whip nor tune;
with coals at three-and-six a sack
laborious toil had fetched a boon.

Yet the coalman nodded knowingly
and whispered his grim philosophy:
Life is a struggle.

Man-Dight was absent from the hill,
his machete rusted with disuse
as ague rocked his steely frame,
his little donkey's teeth went loose.

He died before the oil sheikhs knew
the value of scarce energy,
that oilman, coalman could conspire
to sell the world at any fee.

So even on his death bed, he
groaned his grim philosophy:
Life is a struggle.

MAMA
14.3.1998

Mama, your quiver number was only three,
but you gave milk to many;
the men grew beard,
you still breast-feed them;
women see dem stop sign,
you still don't wean them,
Auntie, Miss Belle, Mama:
good names of yuh deeds them.

You had yuh share of up and down,
hills and ghauts to Gerald Bottom from town.
George Street king-size fire
threatened to burn you;
Hugo blew, he nearly stripped you;
de little dat left,
volcano still grudge you,
but yuh table dun spread
and in yuh four post bed
mosquito cyan moles' you.

Gwarn no, Mama,
nothing here to look back for,
only the carcass of the cattle left
and hungry hounds ready to kill for it.
Don't mind they smile
to camouflage dem guile;
when you were you
you woulda crack de code of dem style.
I trust yuh descendants follow yuh feat:
no accommodation for modern conceit,
blot up a tear in somebody's eye,
fill the mouth of a famished cry.

Gwarn Mama, you pass yuh test.
Gwarn Mama, you deserve yuh rest;
the journey did tedious,
but you had yuh Jesus;
the valley was dark
but He held your hand;
the river was deep,
He was a rock for your feet.
Mek you step over to de golden strand.

Mama, you could hear us,
you could savour the chorus
from yu extended quiver?
'God bless you, Mama',
and the zephyrs echo
across many waters,
'God bless you Mama'.

TEACHER VIO
20.12.2000

Light-hued, with cat-colour eyes,
your background is not truly black –
except from a jaundiced point of view,
through colonizing eyes; and your narrow
nose smells of buccaneer contamination –
the brutish product of harassment higher up.
You had no progeny of blood,
only the heart and brain – and you *midwived*
many, succouring us with pain.
They stand tall who sat well at your feet.
You did not rise to very high degrees
but you were called to handle chiefs
and champions. Lavity Stoutt and Romney,
who won the belt in the Virgin Islands
and a fat purse, still pay you compliments
with sterling words you taught them;
and there are more and lesser lights
in Montserrat whom, like myself,
you illuminated and are pleased to call you
teacher. Missionary at large, you were not
narrowly methodist but methodical
in your approach to teaching. An object
lesson yourself, you showed us how to put
our words in proper places without a bastard
Oxford accent; how to sing in harmony
to the pitch of a tuning fork and used the rod
sparingly whenever we skylarked.
You taught us how to name the bigger islands
and the less, like Jost Van Dyke,
where you sojourned and won national respect.
Wisdom still drops from your lips, light
steals from under the bushel of the Golden
Ages home and I am happy to have seen

your rising. In my journey from the distant
east, the star was bright and I am pleased
to call you teacher; your name is red
between the lines all over my degree.

APPLES FOR THE TEACHER
(For Eileen Edwards 18.10.2000)

Eileen, walk well;
angels will applaud this spell
of duty when you slaked
the children's thirst with a refreshing
cup of learning, washed the dust
of ignorance from their feet
and dried their hurting
with the towel of your care.

Walk well, Eileen;
angels will sum up your slate,
and when they ring the bell
for school reunion up above
there'll be unforbidden apples for the teacher
and supper dressed with love.

UNTITLED TEACHER
Jamaica – 10.8.1999

She looked distracted from a distance.
It was a.m., not quite nine;
too soon to be primed with wine,
too soon for senility.
The lady's lips were moving
the same beat as her feet;
but as we crossed I heard
the lifting burden of her song, not
philosophy or unknown tongues;
the length as modest as her skirt
but albeit arousing. My heart
did not skip a beat but the message
was soul-stirring: 'Thank you God
for food to eat'. I left her, wiser
for the meeting – scarcely meeting –
just a fleeting brush against
my life by an untitled teacher,
but it left a troubling mark.

HE PASSED
11.7.1999

I love to kill mosquitoes
with a heavy hand. It liberates
or rather seems to exorcize
the common murderer in me.

In full view of a flowering light,
this vain mosquito
was looking in my looking glass.
I bopped it hard,

two strokes in one;
I aided destiny;
with little blood it came and passed.
It came to pass

just days after graduation,
this boy prematurely 'qualified'
for his ultimate certificate –
like a bright child who skips class.

Two like lads, who never learnt
how to assuage their common rage,
caressed him with a butcher's hand.
The radio said it touchingly: he passed.

Before the desk, the litmus test
did not add up to murder
or manslaughter. The verdict met
fresh gales of laughter: they had passed.

COLIN HOWARD
6.8.1999

Twice weaned, he won the right
to step into the universe
alone, sporting his own toga
in the leeward of his parents' gaze,
free from their oral 'child companion' –
its 'dated' lore on dating
and *etcetera* instructions.

But there's a tug, a silent chain.
He is not my spitting image
but he fully fits my jeans and shoe
size – same high insteps, spreading toes,
same motifs on his fingernails.
He cannot cancel me where'er he goes;
and his inner fire, the soul's flame,
throws light on the colour of my name.

CONQUEST
1986

Bow to Richards, you northern stars;
panmen, beat his team a roll of honour.

Hitting for the skies,
you brought to earth our dreams,
although your temper on the turf
echoed the pitch of childhood.
Children of the empire,
we did not dream to zero England.

We played in gullies, mountain climes,
brandishing cedars imaging the willow,
trained coconut fronds for guerrilla combat
or pitched battles
on placid English fields.
Children of the empire,
we did not dream to capture lords.

Marching in an epic line of marshals –
Worrell, Sobers, Kanhai, Lloyd –
you infected us with victory,
levelling Montgomery's England.
We shall be generous in glory,
wielding words Great Britain taught us,
send horns of mercy, VSO,
to bring the mother country into line
lest *lesser breeds without the law*
of cricket hit her past the boundary
to decline. Orphan lambs of empire,
we did not think to tame the lion.

Beat the pan for Richards,
stream in praise, you northern stars.

Drunk on dank tobacco leaves,
Warner poisoned us with cane;
your deadly strokes are balm
for the sugar in our brain.
Washing marbled Albion,
you bathed us black with pride.
Children of the empire,
we did not mean to trouble England.

Children of empire,
defend your wicket-gate
from wicked men who batten
on an orange black free state;
we observe the truce
but not declare the innings closed,
we play to win the war.

Bow to Richards, you northern stars
beat a paean, panmen, for his company.

LARA AGAIN
15.12.2000

Lara erupted at play in Adelaide
to bring us Christmas cheer
like an early Santa Claus. He hit
for six the terrorists like Glen McGrath
and wrote his fame again
with hat trick upon hat trick of boundaries.
The West Indies saviour is born again
and runs amok to show it.
And young Marion Samuel, a true disciple,
knows how to shuffle his feet
and follow the beat of the master.
He is no Judas to sell out the game;
I hope he grafts his innings onto Lara's
new beginnings to resurrect our name
from beneath the turf down under at Adelaide.

Lara is a live volcano;
you never know when he will erupt again,
so the Aussies better put their shutters up
if 'the ashes' is to be contained.

TWO MEN ON THE STREATHAM ROAD
1986

1

This island has no ghettoes,
leantos, mass misery,
but man-to-man silent heart-
aches fester painfully.

2

I met an old man on the Streatham road
the other night, head bent low;
over his sagging shoulders sloped
an ancient hoe; his feet
chegwey chegwey in the dazzling bright.
The Nissan train passed him fast like progress
and the promise of politicians,
tractor and plough passed him on the self-same
road and the emigration boat to England.
He was hale and hearty once,
hailed coronation, toasted absent majesty
from a calabash cup, lifted politicians
high above the head of people,
holding all the while his ancient hoe.

3

Eyes against the light, this powerless speaker
carried his own mace on the slippery
road to progress, his hoe a load,
his holdings light as wafer.

4

I met a man on the Streatham road
the other day; the sun was low.
Levite-like I passed him and his hoe,
wondering in the puzzling night
in whose manifesto his fumbling face would show.

5

Man-by-man, silent heart-
aches fester painfully.
I met another man on the Streatham road
the other night, too sick to sleep
in his two-piece pyjama suite,
flimsy as fig leaves;
he was obviously distraught, oblivious
of children laughing loudly at his private
parts making a *pappishow* of misery.
Infants grew to toddlers as he journeyed
on that road, half-step forward, one step
backward, as if his sun stood still.
The old man in the ancient moon,
virile everlastingly, paled with pity
at the plight and flight of brotherhood.

6

I wondered if the old man paid his tithes —
taxes, child supportance, union dues —
whether the gods fined him with this heavy load:
a private nuisance on a crazy road
skirting precipices, hairpin bends,
this feeble euphemism, senior citizen
in one big stride past dotage,
a moving fossil from another age.
In which amendment will he need his rights,
his freedom to be poor, his only guaranteed franchise?

7
I passed him on the other side, wondering:
when my drugged sun drowses in the west
will the church, union, party caucus,
society for the prevention of cruelty
to animals place me on their manifest,
or will I make my second entrance
into childhood with indecent gait?

8
I passed two men the other night
toddling to oblivion on a Christian road.

DEATH OF A BIG MAN
11.5.2002

He was a big man bigger than the metaphor
and with a name like Christopher he has a seat
reserved in higher climes – though namesakes
like Columbus may have silted up the waters.
But if the mariner transgressed, it was for a noble
cause. To float a drowning legacy with a seine
of lies and placate a frowning monarch,
is forgivable. Chris' was well connected.

Also known as Chief and David he was naturally
head of the tribe, head and shoulders taller
than the rest and the *drunken* gods of pentecost
stood ever at his side lacing his words with power.
He could speak fire and brimstone, stock fare
of his faith. And though his voice was gentle
like an unbroken choir boy's in a grey cathedral,
like that other David his slingshots were no toys.

His gifts were prodigal like his girth,
his jacket extra large enwrapped a heart
of gold with just a squeeze. Monuments
to his munificence are many: choice graves
in an up-market lot at Brades, grounds to plant
a clinic in at Cudjoe Head, liberal curves to corner
killer roads at Fogarthy's and a public rule
to sing a song for children in a proper school.

As Santa Claus he was unorthodox.
Without the mask and frigid coat his gifts
were red and warm like blood: choice cuts
of cattle as costly offerings to friendship
and pig scraped clean to lard the liberal
sacrifice (Charles Lamb would love it burnt).

Chris was kind but not indiscriminate.
His junkets were for friends who stayed in line.

Unlike another namesake, the burial garden
is his own and the rock-hewn tomb
prematurely opened as if to lie in state
for two whole days. It was a yawning wound
undressed, biding time to stake the final
claim on a big son of the soil. A forward man
like Christopher will not settle for corruption.
Will he cut a deal with Christ for a snap resurrection?

IN MEMORY
(For a student)

Death came young but it was not beautiful.
A ravenous beak pecked at your liver,
bathing it in blood
dark red like ruby wine.
Your kidney, in kindred toils,
panicked and went out on strike.
The euphemistic doctor (my student too)
stopped the rotting wound with jargon:
renal failure, a tourniquet in words.

I taught you dry imperial measure,
no colony temperance;
you reduced pounds to pence and penny-weights
but lacked common abstinence.
Your death (the doctor said we lost him)
pierced my heart cold as an ice-pick,
my conscience like a knife.
You died of jaundiced education
void of learning fit for life.

ISLAND SON

for Keithroy Maynard

16.1.2002

Like the trinity of terrorist attacks,
your passing froze us in our tracks

on that day when Apple-upon-Hill
was wasted by a winter chill

in Autumn. Trees suddenly lost their leaves
and died, stricken by a new disease.

Birdsong fell strangely silent,
a natural pause to mark the moment

of apocalypse when the Big Apple bit the dust
and professions of in God we trust

rang hollow; when desks of gold turned catafalque,
chic offices commuted to a park

of death. You answered to your country's call
to brave the dance, to spend your all.

In fealty to the tyrant, duty,
you bled to dye the scarlet beauty

of fidelity on the banners of the world
and wear your wounds in front like medals of gold.

Black and white sipped the same cup of sorrow
for a season, suspending till tomorrow

the unreason of American brand apartheid
in the unity of grief when every colour died.

Today the morning blue has left your skies
in starless night. How time flies

faster than spectre planes with a terror crew
of false fanatics drunk on a crazy brew

of righteousness. We drape our flag and write your song
today, and hymn you in your mother tongue.

Tomorrow we shall hail you on another clime
for everlasting tryst, a better harvest time

above September clouds, untimely wintry storms,
no shrill siren, no tuneless fire alarms.

DEAD RESPECT
16.3.2002

After they had sung a hymn about a hill
and trotted out the *rest in peace*
like a tired mantra,
they took the body to a high place
in the field, unleashed a shower of stones
on the dead woman's chest
battering breasts they couldn't tickle yesterday.
One narrowly missed her eyes.
That would have been such a sight
to meet her maker after that pricey
make-up for the grand appearance
dressed in Sunday white.

There is no room to run
from either God or man in that narrow
house; you lie down and take it –
both insult and injury – in a tomb.
The insult began when they let her down –
their trembling feet spread wide
to bridge the deep divide, the ugly breach
in the environment made by a murderous
machine. Nerves were on edge, for fear
they drop the bier and spill her private
circumstance, the ultimate in injuries.

The grave diggers, callous workers,
cavalier gatekeepers of the dead, stole
attention from the mourners with a sideshow
unrehearsed. The comic interludes were staged
in poor taste, especially for someone born
in such a rich estate with the brand name
of a princess, Margaret Rose of Windsor,

(no colour wars with white and off-white roses)
and on their cues for entry, they were wrong.

After the slow dance of the gravediggers
on stubborn clods as stiff as death,
hoes, pick-axes and a mattock borrowed
as an after thought (another class insult),
were press-ganged into service,
and you wonder whether the arrangement for her
journey was as impromptu as their act.
No! no need for a requiem and proxy
penitence, her Most High connection was on track
to yield posthumous dividends
and her sins – if any – not that black.
The final gable was not hip but beautiful,
completely roofed with flowers. A cover up
of dust and ashes with indifferent labour.
You couldn't tag them with industrial action
in an essential service, at the grassroots;
they have their rites. Just a vulgar
show of power. To be paid to push you under
for the world to see is their richest hour.

3: OCCASIONAL POEMS

MEMORIES

Yes man, those were crude times,
those cane-cutting times
when my foot was de plough
and my hand was de harvester
and stout canes would bow
to my murderous machete,
to be robbed of their sugar
to sweeten rich crimes
and my head was de truck,
de tractor and trailor
and my eyes scarce could see
how the dew and the sun
distilled silver droplets
that wept at my feet
in the morningtime grass.
Man, who could forget?

Yes man, those were hard times,
and who could forget?
The clouds bawling tears
to see my skin soaking wet,
de sun burning with rage
to see my pores
pissing sweat
to grow cotton seed
and fertilize greed.

These memories are burnt
deep in my brain,
like the trade marks of slavery
etched in my blood
by steel pens of oppression;
and freedom was choked
in my jugular vein
by coffle and chain.

It will need a revolution
to give mental release,
and a total transfusion
of blood and beliefs
and a brand new psychology
to give my brain ease.
Man, who could forget?

ENTER LENNY
18.11.1999

You would have thought that we had seen it all,
this side of the millennial ball:
Haley's comet, quakes of apocalyptic scale,
a mountain, under the weather, defecating
at both ends, holes without end, too sick to sleep.

A sometime shut-eye fools the doctors
and their formulaic physic; and we denied
our saviours near three times. Night ate light,
bite by crescent bite, in a magic of eclipse.
Cocks crowed out of rhyme and Hugos played the island

in regulation time. Enter Lenny, a little loony,
but dramatic in a late show breaking,
big winds, deep November under wrong direction,
doesn't know west from east, stage right or left,
a choreograph in madness *avec son et lumière.*

A late developer, Lenny moved on a fast track,
he skipped class in the clever sense, pausing
for a disastrous effect like windy orators
while people wait, dying with suspense.
Passing within blood-shot of Jamaica

and under eaves of burglaries in Puerto Rico,
he trained his eye on violence without parental guidance.
The hands of trees were flailing everywhere,
tearing to tatters our wet emotions,
breaching the play rites of Shakespeare.

You toyed with three French men in a sailing saucer
like a cat, cocksure of its prey, playing
at loss and rescue to tickle appetite.
Four locals, call them English, braved the warring straits,
rafting a good neighbour miracle to save the day.

I was fascinated, almost, by your late late show:
Guinness-size waves betting with cliffs at Little Bay;
your video flooding the weather channel;
memory lapses in MONLEC's lighting; but I pause,
a fan of punctuality, I withhold applause.

BEULAH GOATS

Beulah goats
are tramps,
street children of no fixed address.
In their sidewalk
economy
they do drugs
naturally;
they crop forbidden stimulants
from the same tree –
as cheap as sharing needles.

Libertines,
their shepherds have lost face;
they paddock
on the broad highway,
trapped between two churches.
Preachers who molest their rite
with threat of fire
are tailed oft as a pest;
they do not let the false alarm
of some driver's nuisance horn
disturb their quiet rest.

They screw red bulbs
in broad daylight;
footloose,
they walk from man to man
without respect of kin –
no methodist restraint,
no leash of law –
a ram's own child
becomes his dam
stepdaughters, concubines.

Be careful with a mess
of stew from such a tainted flock;
goat water will not pass my throat
without a purifying pill
from Glendon's in-date stock.
I will not be a goat
and have Jah hound me to the left
with addicts, kinks and communists
in His Most High court.

DOVE

1.1.2003

What ill wind or good flew this dove in
on express wing from some alien shore
skirting crosswinds of contention
over the Gerald's port to land
uncannily outside my chamber door
with a baritone moan on new year's morn?
If it presages peace then it is worth
two in the bush and more in the gulf.

The nerve: to invade my family space.
Go chirp your hieroglyph to presidents
and hawkish spouse or to the house
next door. Go scratch a fertile ground
to plant your word and water it with tears.
Make sure it's heard in the red of soufriere
anger. Let it paliate intestine
gripes in politics and, perhaps, in my life?

PARTY

16.8.1999

A few dry cake-crumbs gleaned
by their own industry, no wash down,
and ants will have a party
without the mould of ideology
but liberal with invitations.
Before long you have a throng,
a happy hour like carnival
in Trinidad for a season –
or a Baptist church convention.

But we different.
Must have plate tarts and cakes
of many colours, like a Joseph's coat,
demijohns of mountain dew
and imported water bubbles
just to chase it. Florida chicks
that flew in freshly on the chopper,
flesh of street goats to season
bullish water, ribs briefly dressed
and other mini bites on toothpicks
to tickle appetite.

A motherly handshake of three score and
ten millions can fete us with a difference;
no rigged invitation lists for kick-backs,
no cocktails to corrupt the party,
just a maroon around stout walls
to stave off hydra-headed storms.
When the children's heads are covered
and sweet music in their belly,
only then I'll vote a party.

CRUMBS

14.8.1999

A dog in ancient Israel, whether gentile
or Alsatian, was entitled to the crumbs
from aristocratic tables.

This ordinary undernourished dog,
undergraduate of the Mona campus,
roamed from field to field and narrow

entrances to glean for academic crumbs,
but with underclass success. Donor
dons did not mince their words.

They chewed them over and digested recondite
ideas and brought up bones of big contention.
Little substance was left over.

SOLITUDE
8.4.2000

Solitude is not the delicacy
that it is bruited to be. I do not feel
ashamed to be a lonely, not quite
Londoner. This should have been white meat
for contemplation with fillets
of poetry, delicious blues, rare songs
and an updated *weltanschauung*.

There is no necessary nexus twixt
solitude and art. It might just be rejected –
like the body fights invasion of a foreign
part cut out for its salvation. Poetry
does not thrive on any special diet.
It may infect you in a burial lot
where life is raw with mourning that is
politic or impolite, or when boys lock together
in a cock fight or hooligans at sport.

What philosophy is good taste devoid
of life? What poetry is meet
robbed of the rare blood of the strife?

SPRING HOPE
2.4.2000

From my woollen suite at Park Lane,
British paid (from the arrears), I looked down
on the wintry winds of spring peeling cold
lapels, splitting the scissors of tightly woven
coats, the cocoons of winter. Thinly dressed,
trees in the open park shivered in the breeze.
Spring was green only in the steps of Britons —
except the elderly who had a grey start
on the season and had earned a shuffling
handicap from an earlier whistle
of the wind. Springless too were the dour faces
of Montserratians plumbing the reason
mother was so cold in their sunless season.

I looked down on white Britons for a season
parrying the whims of spring with black
umbrellas like distended bowler hats.
Faces tightly drawn, hands cuffed in pockets,
they only break the cloak of silence
for a maniac laugh into the ears of walking telephones
whose ripples radiate grave suspicion.
Living in Rome, brollies of Montserratians also
mushroom; like Brits their ears sprout telephones.
Hailstones rain like pumice but no mangoes
fall. With cold ash carpeting their feet
their heart skips a tectonic beat and they affect
to feel at home. Hope springs...

A RICH PLACE
14.4.2000

Unfinished island, Gibraltar is a bit big
for its size; too many men for miles, too many wheels
for co-existence without a rub; two mothers, two head-
quarters. It has the malady of inbetweenity.
It is a rock between a rock and the hard face
of Spain still bruised from the collision of Utrecht.
It feels the heavy weight of Spain in an uneven
contest, while the mother tongue is silent at ringside
and England is content to turn a blind eye,
continentally. It is a rich place with shops that shout
'real English fish and chips' once you get past
the strong crosswinds of history or crawl beyond
the maddening Madrid wall. A rich land, limestone really,
off Europe and off-white, draped with its own anaemic
shade of green; a rock that grows palaces and cannons,
hills of *petits pains*, rivers of wine – insurances
against a shortage of communion save with the
Pretender who will not stoop to break bread
with a force-ripe colony or come to court to settle in
a juvenile divorce; a place rich with the resonance of war
and rumours of unarmed words. It is a luxurious
rock. Birds of many schools and pedigree sun-bathe
atop the rock or swirl in shifts of non-stop
motion in an aerial display or swim like fishes
in a sky-blue ocean. There is no Oxford Street
where cardboard blankets fret your feet, but a tailless
ape, a stunted Darwin specimen, conspires
to take your bread to fatten greed and coexistence,
aping the tired idiom of diplomacy.
The temperate caves do not grow ice, but dark grey
spines of stalactites hang stoutly from the concave

canopy in gothic grace – fit furniture for the pillars
of Hercules where myth and history mingle
to decorous effect. Michael Cave is an awesome place.

Hailing from a lesser league of colonies
that feel the mite of England and the right
to relegation after failing the mean test,
I was impressed to hear echoes
of the cannon's hollow roar in a rich place.
It was hard to leave the Rock between a rock
and a hard place. Not that you are so attached in spite of
first-sight love, but contrary winds blow there against
the taking off, and England chuckles while Spain laughs.

VIRGINS CELEBRATE
19.11.2000

The virgin islands are in celebration mode;
(now hardly virgins) they have exchanged
their maidenhead for mammon and who wouldn't
if you had the contours, curves in the right
places, voluptuous coves, and with Delilah's
winning wiles you are able to deliver the goods.
The vacation menu excites today, a pot-
pourri of action, so no need to gamble
on potluck, though that can be ecstatic too.

There is no fifty-gun salute but a peacetime
armada of pleasure boats clap the uneven
chain of islands in polite applause. No panoply
of war planes in artistic drill formation,
but black birds in lyrical flight parade and pirouette
overhead in an unrehearsed display, without
the academic freight of import substitution,
just an innate sense of duty. No trumpets brag and bray
the bloodless restoration of the people's rule
but hillside houses gloat at the pleasing prospects
in the Valley Road in tune with the off-beat
bass of backhoe and bobcat mining a new entrepot,
and distant merchant ships, pot-bellied
with container cargoes, steam into the harbour
to feed a beehive of activities.

There is no Arlington or stout redoubt
to harbour ghosts of the resistance,
but they came from tribulation just the same,
and penance of imperial penury
in salt trenches and on guerilla cattle hills.
So they can call a party rich with saffron
rice (a mire of gravy on the side) and bread

heavily larded like a bad chest cold,
they murmur polite amens to the parson
preaching unity to both sides of the aisle;
sit polite through speeches liberal
with self-congratulations from colonized
and colonizer. The latter still gives
and takes away; blessed be the name
of the lord now that the feud is nearly over.

Today is coronation day; virgins unveil
brazen native busts brassiered in the union jack,
sing silken words to save the Queen,
salvage local heroes to rescue them from dust,
burying bygones in their stead; but budding
virgins can't forget the seven-fold
foreign threat to rob them of their launderette
with loads of lucre in the wash.

The sun in orange light enters from a curtain
of grey cumulus to gild the heroic holiday;
its duty run, it will hum a soft doxology
before the evening dive routine into
the rejoicing sea, until tomorrow's restoration.
The Virgin Islands are in party mood today
and, loyal to the stereotype, are oblivious
of time. You adjust to avoid a fit
and since they bid me celebrate, my only other angst
is to be a fit, not just a willing, virgin mate.

STOP CLOCK
(For Eudora 8.4.2000)

At the creditable score of B plus years,
common things take on uncommon countenance --
like that clock cut out like Montserrat,
wedded to the dining wall these thirty years,
ticking the loyal tock, though soufriere's domes
and marriages collapse, losing rhythm and rhyme,
becoming scarred like bad grammar in an essay.

It was our wedding present from the school.
We are lucky that the marriage banquet
board still satisfies through tickings off,
the occasional alarm, the ups and downs of hands
in constant round to harmonize clockwise
motions and counter-clock emotions.
Your single-minded duty puts us to shame;
no extravagant protestation, just a metallic tick
between a silent hieroglyph of numbers.

You did not escape the rust of the environment
and your faded figures hint of dusk;
your tired limbs will one day freeze
unheralded by arthritis. Out of breath,
your tick will suddenly stop. And ours?
Who will remain to raise the first alarm?
But after a bond of thirty years, who really cares?

MOTHER'S DAY POEM
8.5.2000

I'll be a sceptic on this mother's day;
I won't bake oily bakes for breakfast
with purple boulanger; no diabetic
icing on the cake with cold and crooked words.
I'll rob no flower bed or rape a sickly rose
by rupturing its red light hedge of thorns
and cut its prime-time beauty to decorate
the spawns of Eve, both quick and dead. I'll pick
a sinful apple instead, one green with memory.
I'll leave the greeting to designing cards
from England and the USA, their wash of trade
in words (one way) sweet and facile, so
like drinking water on a thirsty day,
a male flirt kissing toes or fat mud fed to pigs.

But how to tell love from the heart except
with word or hand, I do not know. I'll copycat
the vulgar, and say 'I love you so'.

PILGRIMAGE
25.12.2000

Today we make our annual *pilgrimage*
to the hospital. The newly baptized word
gives sanctity to visits. We have lost
the ancient name of Glendon
but 'St. John's', annointed with divinity,
is most appropriate if we overlook
denominational bias for a season.
The Governor and helpmeet will be there;
this gives a little whiteness to the Christmas,
though it is not politic to say so
but I will plead poetic licence if it's warranted
to speak uneasy verities.

We bear healthy tidings for the patients
and partly good appearances,
but there's a zeal about our pilgrimage this year –
apart from Kuttè's new maracas art.
It is His Excellency's eve of permanent leave
and the Ministers' music comes
from heart-strings with a fervent wish
for five more re-appearances after the election.
All in all it was a profitable event
with yuletide currency wisely spent.

RETIREMENT
26.6.2000

There is a shadowy ring
about retirement;
it smacks of sunset
nightness
dark
cold and loneliness
in a parking lot.

Better to leave the bout
before my legs pull out
from under me;
better to leave the ring
before the sting
is taken from my punch;
better to leave
while the referee still holds up my hand
before the left hook of arthritis lands,
before my head gets soft with blows,
hot ague shakes me to my toes,
before my piston skips a beat,
I'll quit.
Better bow out now
before boxers and bearers
take me out.

TO CALL ME SIR

A liberal Queen has lately sent her messenger
with a white paper to pin on me a Sir
on hearsay evidence, like borrowed charges
on the heads of slaves in an unholy dispensation.
In this case the elders nod their approbation;
and children at my bearded knee have beat her
to the call, dubbing me Sir out of respect and fear,
for the tongue of her Britannic majesty
dictates that they salute me Sir, in letter at least
since all my silent parts spout masculinity.

Ghosts have left the shadows at Long Ground
and Hermitage to rock the arena with applause.
Gerald's Bottom rings with echoes. The siren
is silent, leaving spirits free to rattle rustic
instruments to guild the rising of an eastern son
at evening. In local loyalty and lowly protocol
they weave loblolly branches instead of stately palms.

The bright sword surprised me. I learnt of
green knights only, and black princes who were white
in clumsy coats of mail. A black Montserratian
(k)night was the provision garden of my mother's life
or a silent spelling catch for little boys
sweating English out behind the sovereign's back
on grey slates and penitential benches.

I hope the graft succeeds, to patch a Saxon scion
to a green stem grown behind God's back
in a rural *cul-de-sac*. Pregnant clouds assemble
overhead. I know not if to dampen or to bless
the rising. Crab gaulin counsels trust no cloud
of saffron, black or white: a wise light
from the east. Living voices are standing up
all over the pavilion, joining branches
with the dead at Long Ground and Hermitage
to still the hungry voices of a lean minority.
Gerald's and like-minded Bottoms murmur with the echoes.

DECISION
8.5.2002

It is a sticky choice to make. No prime
time summit such as whether to attack
the women of Iraq for loyalty to moguls

right or left. It is not like planting
your own puppet prince with pipelines to America
for bombs and crude intelligence

or at what beach a plane should dock
to avoid the cross-winds of contention
when landing on the rock of Montserrat.

It is a new database dilemma:
commissioning an address book – ejecting
worthless tenants. More like a voters' manifest.

To be fair, the dead should go in order to arrest
corruption, although a little sad to cancel
loyal memories with an unfeeling hand.

I must not lightly disenfranchise friends
whose thoughts no longer correspond
with mine and do not toast my party.

In a democracy, contrary winds are free
to blow against my craft. This is an absolute.
I only draw the line to overthrow

passengers and yes people. I'll suspend
sentence lest I damn the innocent. Offenders
of the faith deserve a space for penitence

just like defenders of the likes of Charles
who get away with murder, by metaphor I mean
and a princely latitude for reconcilement.

This version of to be or not to be is burdensome.
Death and new birth always come with pain.
I'll settle for the up-to-date and people with a name.

NOTES

'Volcano Watch' p. 16
Chances peak (3002 feet) was, until the growth of volcanic domes, the highest mountain in the island. Generally the eruption occurred at Chances Soufriere.

expressions is a creole word for expletives or 'bad words'.

'Volcano Vespers' p. 21
Tar River and Long Ground, the districts nearest to the volcano, were the first to feel its might in 1995.

'A Minute Silence' p. 22
freco or fresco, crushed ice with a syrup, is also known as sno(w)-cone.

CARICOM, the acronym for Caribbean Community and Common Market.

'Paradise Again?' p. 27
Olveston: a village in England where the humanitarian Joseph Sturge grew up. He gave the name to one of the many estates which he purchased in Montserrat in the nineteenth century.

tonton macoute and *mongoose gang* refer to special soldiers specially trained to guard the rulers in Haiti and Grenada respectively, in an earlier time.

'DFID' p. 30
DFID is the acronym for Department for International Development (Clare Short was the then Minister).

'A Little Lonely' p. 31
Old Towne and Olveston contain palatial buildings owned to a great extent by expatriates. They were developed during a real estate boom in the 1960s.

'September 17' p. 33
September 17 is an uncanny date in Montserrat. A major plane crash occurred on that date; hurricane Hugo devastated Montserrat on the 17th; and it was also the date of one of the major eruptions.

'Beloved Island' p. 36
The neighbouring Anglophone island of Antigua is not just Montserrat's main connection with the outside world but the place where islanders shop, often at the expense of the local commercial community.

'Mission' p. 37
Opale Express is the ferry chartered by the British for passenger traffic between Montserrat and Antigua. There is also a helicopter which carries eight persons.

'Volcano Audit' p. 43
Cat boil: In folk belief, if you give a gift and take it back, you will be infected with cat boils, meaning a painful swelling of the skin.

'Teacher Vio' p. 53
Lavity Stoutt and Cyril Romney, former Chief Ministers of the British Virgin Islands, were taught by Viola Norman of Farms, Montserrat, as was this author.

'He Passed' p. 57
certificate was a mis-pronounciation associated with unlearned persons.

'Conquest' p. 59
Richards is Vivian Richards (now Sir) a famous cricketer who captained the West Indies team with resounding success.

Warner is Thomas Warner the man who colonized the British Leeward Islands.

'Lara Again' p. 61
Glen McGrath, an Australian bowler has repeatedly claimed the wicket of star West Indian batsman, Brian Lara.

'Two Men on the Streatham Road' p. 62
chegwey is a creole word which means to move in an ungainly manner.

pappishow is a creole word for a ridiculous, funny or embarrassing situation or even a person.

'Death of a Big Man' p. 65
David Christopher Fenton, prominent island politician and businessman, demonstrated his friendship and favour at Christmastime with gifts of meat. He also gave sites in his burial ground at Brades to the chosen. This folk hero of fundamentalist faith was called Chris, or is it Chris(t)?

'Enter Lenny' p. 77
MONLEC is the acronym for Montserrat Electricity Company.

'Beulah Goats' p. 79
Glendon is the name of the abandoned public hospital in Plymouth.

'Crumbs' p. 83
Mona is the Jamaican campus of the University of the West Indies.

'A Rich Place' p. 86
Utrecht: Gibraltar's ownership problems with Spain stem from arrangements made between England and Spain at the treaty of Utrecht in 1713.

'Virgins Celebrate' p. 88
The British Virgin Islands lost their legislative council, their instrument of self-government in 1902, and regained it in 1950. In 2000 they celebrated the half-century of semi-self-government with pomp and ceremony.

'Mother's Day Poem' p. 91
boulanger is the eggplant, aubergine or antrover.

'Pilgrimage' p. 92
Kuttè is a local 'character' with a low IQ.

ALSO BY HOWARD A. FERGUS
FROM PEEPAL TREE

Lara Rains and Colonial Rites
ISBN 0-948833-95-5   88 pages   1998   £6.95

Howard Fergus's poems explore the nature of living on Montserrat, a 'two-be-three island/hard like rock', vulnerable to the forces of nature (Hurricane Hugo and the erupting Soufriere) and still 'this British corridor'. He writes honestly and observantly about these contingencies, finding in them metaphors for experiences which are universal. Nature's force strips life to its bare essentials ('Soufriere opened a new bible/in her pulpit in the hills/ to teach us the arithmetic of days') and reveals creation and destruction as one ('We celebrate Hugo child of God/ he killed and made alive for a season').

In a small island society, individual lives take on an enhanced significance: they are its one true resource and the sequence of obituary poems brings home with especial force how irreplaceable they are. Beyond Montserrat, Fergus looks for a wider Caribbean unity, but finds it only in cricket (and crime). Cricket, indeed, provides a major focus for his sense of the ironies of Caribbean history: that through a white-flannelled colonial rite with its roots in an imperial sense of Englishness, the West Indies has found its only true political framework and the means, explored in the sequence of poems celebrating Brian Lara's feats of 1994, to overturn symbolically the centuries of enslavement and colonialism.

ABOUT THE AUTHOR

Sir Howard A. Fergus was born at Long Ground in Montserrat. He attended Montserrat Grammar School, Erdiston Teacher's College in Barbados, the University College of the West Indies, the Universities of Bristol and Manchester, and finally UWI (Ph. D, 1978).

He has served Montserrat since 1955 as a teacher, voucher clerk, Chief Education Officer (1970-73), Acting Permanent Secretary, and from 1975, Speaker of the Montserrat Legislative Council and De Facto Deputy Governor from 1976. Since 1974 his main job has been that of Extra-Mural Resident Tutor at UWI, Montserrat, where he ran a Creative Writing Workshop. He was awarded an CBE in 1995 and knighted in 2001 for his outstanding sevices to Montserrat. He is one of the few to have remained on the island since the devastating eruption of Soufriere in 1997. As well as being 'a poet of real stature' (Stewart Brown, Longman *Caribbean New Voices*), Fergus is Montserrat's official historian and has written extensively about the island.